MONSTERS
YOU NEVER HEARD OF

MONSTERS
YOU NEVER HEARD OF

Daniel
Cohen

Illustrated with photographs
and prints

DODD, MEAD & COMPANY
NEW YORK

To the young Edward

Printed in the United States of America

1 2 3 4 5 6 7 8 9 10

Library of Congress Cataloging in Publication Data

Cohen, Daniel.
Monsters you never heard of.

Includes index.
SUMMARY: Accounts of lesser-known monsters, including the Jersey Devil, Hairy Hands, Dover Demon, Spring-Heeled Jack, and other phantom animals.
1. Monsters—Juvenile literature. 2. Animals, Legends and stories of—Juvenile literature.
[1. Monsters. 2. Animal lore] I. Title.
QL89.C64 001.9'94 79-23641
ISBN 0-396-07789-7

CONTENTS

1

THE WORLD OF MONSTERS

Monsters—they frighten us and they fascinate us.

People have probably always been like that. You can imagine people thousands of years ago sitting around a campfire at night. They hear noises out there in the darkness, just beyond the light of the fire. What is it? A harmless animal? A dangerous animal? Perhaps it is something strange and terrible and completely unknown—a monster.

Of course, people would be afraid. They would imagine all kinds of terrible and terrifying creatures. Everyone would want to know what was out there. But very few would be brave enough to go out into the dark and try to find the thing.

Today we are more fascinated by monsters than frightened by them. We might feel differently if we thought we were going to meet one in the woods. But as long as we are safe at home, most of us like to believe in monsters. It would be boring to think that science has been able to identify and classify every large animal on earth. It is far more exciting to believe that there still are strange, terrifying, and unknown things out there somewhere.

Creatures like Bigfoot and the Loch Ness monster are well known. But there are many other monsters that some people believe exist now, or have existed not too long ago. These monsters just have not received the right publicity.

Here, for your education and entertainment, are accounts of a dozen of these lesser-known monsters—monsters you probably never heard of before.

These monsters are a mixed group. They

range from a 115 foot-long snake with glowing eyes to a winged thing in the pine woods of New Jersey, and from something that might have been human and hopping around London in Queen Victoria's day to something that might be a kangaroo hopping around Chicago in our own day. These monsters range from creatures that are quite down to earth, and ordinary—for monsters—to creatures that seem out of this world.

All of these accounts are "told as true." That is, they are reports of what was supposed to have actually happened. They are not just stories made up to frighten and amuse people.

I warn you, however, if you are looking for hard evidence that any of these creatures exist, you are not going to find very much of it here, because there isn't very much. Most monsters have proved to be extremely hard to catch, and these are no exception.

But then, if we could catch them and classify them, they really wouldn't be monsters anymore, would they?

2

THE JERSEY DEVIL

Right in the middle of one of the most thickly populated areas in the United States are the New Jersey Pine Barrens. The Pine Barrens are about 1,700 square miles of trees, sandy soil, and not much else.

Not many people live in the Pine Barrens. About 150 years ago iron was mined there. But it was poor quality iron and could not compete with better iron found in other places. The mines closed down. Some people moved away. The small number of people who do live in this region today are poor and isolated.

From the Pine Barrens come tales of a monster called the Jersey Devil.

The earliest tales of the Jersey Devil date back to colonial times. According to one legend, the Jersey Devil was the monstrous offspring of a woman known only as Mother Leeds. The creature is also called, among other things, the Leeds Devil.

Mother Leeds had a dozen children and didn't want any more. When she discovered she was going to have another one, she said, "I am tired of children! Let it be a devil!" And, according to the legend, it was. After it was born the monstrous thing escaped up the chimney and hid out in the Pine Barrens.

There are many other versions of this story. But this one is the most common.

Whatever its origin, by the middle of the nineteenth century a lot of people thought there was some sort of monster living in the Pine Barrens.

There have been many different descriptions of the Jersey Devil. In general, the descriptions say the monster has a body like a kangaroo, a head like a horse, wings like a bat, horselike or piglike feet, and a forked or pointed tail.

Above and opposite: Views of the Jersey Devil that appeared in a Philadelphia newspaper during the 1909 scare.

That description makes the Jersey Devil sound like a joke. But it was no joke. During the nineteenth century a lot of people reported seeing the thing.

Others said they could hear its terrible screams in the woods. Strange footprints were found. The Jersey Devil was even accused of killing large numbers of chickens and sheep. Many people in the Pine Barrens were really afraid of it. They didn't like to go out after dark.

Outsiders thought "the Pineys," as the people of the Pine Barrens were sometimes called, were just superstitious. Late in the nineteenth century one man predicted that "with the advent of the new century," belief in the monster would die out. He was as wrong as he could be.

In the week of January 16 to 23, 1909, the Jersey Devil left the Pine Barrens and wandered around more populated regions surrounding the Barrens. The Devil or its footprints were seen by thousands. Many of those who reported seeing the creature were highly respected members of their communities.

There was, for example, E. W. Minster, the postmaster of Bristol, New Jersey. Minster was a light sleeper. At about two o'clock in the morning of January 17, 1909, he was awakened by a strange noise. He looked out his window, just in time to see the Jersey Devil fly past.

"Its head resembled that of a ram, with curled horns, and its long thick neck was thrust forward in flight. It had long thin wings and short legs, the front legs shorter than the hind. Again, it uttered its mournful and awful call—a combination of a squawk and a whistle, the beginning very high and piercing and ending very low and hoarse . . ."

On Thursday of that fateful week all the passengers on a late night trolley car going from Clementon to Camden, New Jersey, saw the thing circling overhead. The conductor, Lewis Boeger, later described what he had seen:

"In general appearance it resembled a kangaroo . . . It has a long neck and from what glimpse I got of its head its features were hideous. It has wings of a fairly good size and of course in the darkness looked black. Its legs are long and somewhat slender and were held in just such a position as a swan's when it is flying. We all tried to get a look at its feet to see what shape they were but the darkness was too great. It looked to be about four feet high."

There were hundreds of such reports in the newspapers throughout the area.

Then there were the footprints. The prints looked like the hoofprints of a small pony. They seemed to be all over the place. Some even appeared on the tops of roofs.

People were genuinely frightened. Many would not go out at night. Children were kept home from school. Hunting parties were organized. Many people claimed to have shot at the thing. There were even reports that it had been killed or captured. The reports turned out to be false.

Then, just as mysteriously as the Jersey Devil scare began, it ended.

While people stopped seeing the Jersey Devil, interest in the monster remained high. The Philadelphia Zoo offered a $10,000 reward for the capture of the creature. The Zoo director didn't really believe in the Devil. He said, "Undoubtedly it could draw crowds to the [zoo] and would be of educational value too—if it exists. But my private opinion is that it is going to be very hard to capture."

There were plenty of hoaxes too. A couple of showmen named Jacob F. Hope and Norman Jefferies created their own Jersey Devil. They rented a large kangaroo, and fixed a set of false wings on its back. They painted green stripes

An advertisement for the Jersey Devil hoax created by Hope and Jefferies.

on the animal. Then they put it on exhibit in Philadelphia. People had to pay a dime to get a quick look at it. Jefferies later admitted his part in the hoax.

After the one amazing week in January, 1909, sightings of the Jersey Devil dropped off sharply. But people still reported seeing the strange creature, from time to time. There was a regular Jersey Devil panic in Gibbstown, New Jersey, in 1951. Some children saw the "thing" from the window of their clubhouse at the edge of town. A group of teenagers went out in the woods to hunt for it. One said that the thing nearly caught him. Many people reported hearing "shrill, unearthly screams" in the woods.

The chief of police searched the area but found nothing. The children at the Gibbstown schools were so excited that the principal called the chief of police for help. The chief was also getting a lot of calls from frightened residents and from curious outsiders. Finally, he got fed up. He posted signs all around town which read: THE JERSEY DEVIL IS A HOAX.

Still, people report seeing it and hearing it.

Local officials try to put down a Jersey Devil scare in Gibbstown in 1951.

When chickens are killed or dogs disappear, there are always those who say, "The Jersey Devil did it."

What was, or is, the Jersey Devil?

Of course, no one really knows, but there are plenty of theories. The most probable one is that the whole thing is a case of mass hysteria.

Others think that the legend has some beginning in reality. Perhaps there really was a "Mother Leeds" or someone like that. She may have had a deformed child. At one time such children were kept hidden away. Perhaps this unfortunate child ran away and lived in the dense woods of the Pine Barrens. He may never have been seen clearly. He may have lived by raiding farms and isolated houses. Wild stories would have grown up around such a person.

Another theory is that the legend started when people encountered a large and unfamiliar bird. There is something rather birdlike about many of the descriptions of the Jersey Devil. The bird might have been a sandhill crane, which was once common in New Jersey.

The sandhill crane stands about four feet tall.

It has a violent temper when cornered, and can chase away a man. There are rumors that people have actually been killed by the bird's long bill driven through the eye into the brain.

There is no shortage of theories to explain the Jersey Devil. None can be proved, or disproved.

In recent years there have not been too many sightings of the Jersey Devil. Perhaps the whole legend of the Jersey Devil will just fade away. But I will not predict that it will. Less than one hundred years ago someone else made that prediction and he was dead wrong.

3

SPRING-HEELED JACK

In 1888, London was terrified by a series of mysterious murders. The killer was never caught. This unknown murderer was given the name Jack the Ripper.

A half century earlier an even more mysterious Jack was terrorizing London. This creature—no one seemed quite sure what it was—was given the name Spring-Heeled Jack.

Rumors about the creature began late in 1837. There were many different descriptions, each one wilder than the one before. The thing was said to look vaguely like a powerfully built man. Some said it had wings, or horns, or that it breathed flames. But one thing that everybody said about the creature was that it jumped. It would jump out at women, usually at night. It was never reported to have killed anyone, but it did terrify its victims. Then it would jump away. It could make tremendous leaps, clearing fences and trees in a single bound. That is how it got the name Spring-Heeled Jack.

The police heard about some of these attacks, but they did not take them seriously. One day, early in 1838, the official attitude changed. A very respectable-looking gentleman, accompanied by a young woman, came to the police station in Lambeth Street. The man said that he and his two daughters lived in Bearbind Lane, at that time an isolated spot on the outskirts of London.

He said that on the previous night one of his daughters went to answer a ring at the gate. Outside the gate stood a tall man. She could not make the figure out too well because it was dark and foggy and the man was wrapped in a cloak. The man said he was a policeman. Then he said that he had just caught Spring-Heeled

Jack. "For God's sake, bring a light," he cried.

The girl ran to the house and got a lighted candle. She gave it to the cloaked figure. Suddenly he threw back his cloak, revealing a "hideous and frightful appearance." He seemed to be wearing a helmet, and a shiny white suit. He slashed at her with metalic claws, tearing her dress. Blue and white flames shot from his mouth. Naturally, the girl screamed. The screams brought people running, but the creature bounded away before anyone else could get a look at him.

The police combed the area but found nothing.

A few months later a butcher named Sales came to the Lambeth Street police station. He said that on the previous evening his two sisters had been attacked by a cloaked creature. The thing squirted blue flames at the face of the younger girl. She had been frightened half to death.

Many people were frightened. They demanded that the police protect them. But protect them against what? No one seemed to know.

There was a report that a strange and ghastly-looking creature had been seen climbing the spire of a London church. It spent several minutes glaring at the crowd below before leaping from its high perch and disappearing into the darkness. The same sort of creature had also been reported climbing the Tower of London.

Reports of this kind always bring out the hoaxers. In Warwickshire police caught a young man with springs attached to his boots, and wearing a sheet and mask.

Stories about Spring-Heeled Jack soon began appearing in "penny dreadfuls." These were cheap publications that sold for a penny. Stories in the "penny dreadfuls" were fiction, and highly sensationalized fiction at that. Still, "penny dreadfuls" were very popular, particularly among the poor, who could not afford any other type of reading matter.

The Spring-Heeled Jack of the "penny dreadfuls" was not an evil monster. He was a strange-looking superhero. He was a bit like the popular comic book hero, the Hulk. Amid flashes of lightning and rolls of thunder he would arrive to frighten some evil-doer.

Cover for a "penny dreadful" story about *Spring-Heeled Jack, the Terror of London.*

Spring-Heeled Jack stories kept on appearing for years. In 1863 there was a very popular play in London called "Spring-Heeled Jack; or the Felon's Wrongs." It and several other Spring-Heeled Jack plays ran for several seasons. All of this indicated the public's general fascination with the subject.

The "real" Spring-Heeled Jack was still reported from time to time. In the 1860s there was an outbreak of Spring-Heeled Jack sightings around London. According to one report, the monster had been cornered by an angry mob but got away by jumping over a hedge. People kept their children off the streets for fear of running into the thing.

In 1878, Spring-Heeled Jack was reported in the town of Aldershot. An athletic army officer was arrested for impersonating the monster, but the charge appears to have been false.

From time to time mysterious footprints, or what seem to be footprints, are found in different parts of the world. In February, 1855, a great number of these mysterious footprints were found in the snow over a wide area of

Devonshire in England. Trails of prints stretched for miles and then ended abruptly. Prints were even found on the tops of houses.

No one saw the thing that made the prints. No one could explain what had made them either. Skeptics didn't think they were prints at all. They thought the marks were the result of melting snow and overactive imaginations. Someone suggested that a kangaroo might have gotten loose from a zoo.

An awful lot of people said that the marks were really the hoofprints of the Devil himself. And then there were a few who suggested that it was just Spring-Heeled Jack, up to his old tricks once again.

4
PHANTOM ANIMALS

Lions, tigers, or pumas are not monsters when they are found in the jungle or the zoo. But when they are found roaming around central Illinois or the English countryside and no one can figure out how they got there, then it seems that something strange is going on. It is stranger still when those creatures appear and disappear mysteriously. They always get away from the people who set out to hunt them.

Normally, kangaroos are not very frightening. But what about a mysterious kangaroo in the middle of Chicago that is strong enough to beat up a couple of policemen? Or a giant kangaroo in the middle of Tennessee that kills dogs and chickens? Like the mysterious giant cats, those kangaroos seem able to appear and disappear at will.

The mysterious cats and kangaroos are just some of the world's "phantom animals." There are a large number of reported encounters with phantom animals. Such reports go back a long way and continue right up to the present day. They come from many different parts of the world.

We can start with an 1823 account of a "tiger" that was seen around Russelville, Kentucky. The creature was supposed to be huge. One man said that it had the largest eyes he had ever seen in any animal.

Local residents went out hunting the thing. Many of them were excellent marksmen. Several times they got close enough to get off good shots at it, but no one ever seemed able to hit it. At last report the "tiger" was seen heading off in the direction of Tennessee.

A young woman named Mary Crane had a frightening and strange experience in December, 1877. She lived on a farm near the village of Sun, Indiana. There had been a report of "some monstrous animal" prowling around in the woods near the village.

One night Mary had to go into the village. She was afraid to go alone. She asked a young man from a nearby farm to go with her.

As they were walking through the woods they heard an awful shriek behind them. They turned to see a pair of glowing eyes, not more than forty feet away. The pair ran off down the road as fast as they could. When they looked back they could see something, "big as a good-sized calf, with a tail as long as a door," running after them.

The young man was the faster runner. He bolted on ahead into the village. Mary Crane was left alone. The thing got close enough to rip at her dress with its claws. That was too much, and she fainted.

When she woke up she was on the ground, and something was licking her face. She just kept her eyes shut and prayed. Soon she heard voices coming from the village. The creature let out a shriek, and bounded back into the woods.

Phantom lions have often been reported in the United States and Great Britain.

The thing was hunted for days afterward. But nothing was found except the footprints of an unknown animal.

In 1917 a mysterious big cat was reported in central Illinois. Local people nicknamed it "Nellie the Lion." Several people had reported seeing something that looked like "an African lion." The most dramatic incident took place on July 29. Two families from Decatur, Illinois, were driving west on Springfield Road at about 10:30 in the evening. The lion jumped from the tall grass alongside the road onto the car. Then it slid off and ran away.

There were a number of hunts conducted for Nellie. Several dogs were shot by accident. One man shot at a car, when he mistook the headlights for Nellie's glowing eyes. But Nellie herself vanished as mysteriously as she had appeared.

On April 10, 1970, a man named Mike Busby of Cairo, Illinois, claimed that he was actually attacked by a giant black cat, probably a black panther. There were other reports of a black panther in the region. A local newspaper noted

Drawing of a puma, or mountain lion. Is it the phantom cat?

that reports of a strange black panther in the area had been coming in for years. No one had ever been able to find the creature, however.

Now, about this time you may be thinking, perhaps these people *did* meet real, large cats. The mountain lion or puma is native to the United States. The puma, however, either never lived in, or has long been gone from, the places where these phantom cat reports have been made. Of course, it is always possible that a stray puma could account for some of the reports. But the possibility is a small one.

African lions, tigers, and black panthers are

not at all native to the United States. But what if one escaped from a nearby zoo or circus? Whenever a phantom cat is reported, that suggestion comes up at once. Local authorities always check out the possibility. But escaped lions and tigers are very rare. There is no case in which an escaped animal can be linked to the phantom cat sightings.

Phantom cat sightings are perhaps even more common in Great Britain than in the United States. The best known of these is the Surrey puma or Surrey lion. The thing has been sighted regularly in the district of Surrey since the early 1960s. The sightings have been so frequent that one local newspaper complained recently about the "summer ritual of puma spotting."

Usually the Surrey puma has been reported as a large growling and menacing creature. But there is one odd report in which the creature is said to have behaved like—well, like a real pussycat. On September 1, 1966, a woman was walking through a thistle patch in Hampshire (near Surrey). She stepped on the tail of a

puma. The animal reared up on its hind legs and struck out at her with both its paws. The woman was not frightened. She picked up a stick and hit the creature on the nose. That so frightened the beast that it ran up a tree. The woman went for help, but when she came back the thing was gone.

On October 14, 1977, a group of workers near Reigate in Surrey saw the thing repeatedly. One of them even managed to take a picture of it. But the creature was too far away for a good picture. It might have been a puma in the photograph. On the other hand, it might only have been a large house cat.

The Surrey puma has never been found. But since it seems to be a regular visitor, it will almost certainly be back again.

Not to be outdone, the district of Nottingham has its own phantom cat. It is called the Nottingham lion.

The story of the Nottingham lion began early

The Surrey puma is Britain's most persistent phantom animal. This is a real puma.

in the morning of July 29, 1976. Two milkmen were making their rounds near the entrance to the Nottingham airport. They both saw what they were sure as a lion—". . . its head down and its long tail had a bushy end. It was walking slowly away from us."

They watched it walk around the edge of a field and then called the police. The story got in the newspapers. Over the next week or so there were sixty or more sightings of the Nottingham lion.

The police checked all the zoos and private animal collections within a hundred miles. No one had lost a lion. A massive search was carried out. Dogs and even a helicopter were used in the search.

At first, the police were quite sure there was a loose lion. But as the search went on and they found nothing, they became discouraged. Finally, the police became convinced that the whole thing was a mistake.

It wasn't a real lion at all. It was just another one of the world's phantom cats.

America is not only infested by phantom cats,

it also has phantom kangaroos. Mysterious kangaroos have regularly been reported hopping around various parts of the United States for nearly a century now.

The first known account of a phantom kangaroo comes from the town of New Richmond, Wisconsin, in 1900. There, a Mrs. Glover said that she saw a kangaroo hopping through a neighbor's backyard in the middle of a storm.

Local people remembered that the year before a circus stopping in the town had nearly been destroyed by a tornado. At first, everyone assumed that the kangaroo was an escaped circus animal. But the circus owners denied that they had lost a kangaroo. In fact, they said they never even owned a kangaroo. Besides, it is unlikely that any kangaroo could have survived a Wisconsin winter.

That same year, in Mays Landing, New Jersey, a woman named Amanda Sutts saw "this thing that looked like a kangaroo. It wasn't such a big animal—it was about the size of a small calf and weighed about 150 pounds." Mrs. Sutts thought she had seen the famous Jersey

Devil. If you will recall, the Jersey Devil was often described as looking like a kangaroo. When a showman wanted to display a phony Jersey Devil, he used a kangaroo with wings attached to its back.

In January, 1934, a strange creature was seen in the small community of South Pittsburgh, Tennessee. Reverend W. J. Handcock said, "It was fast as lightning and looked like a giant kangaroo running and leaping across the field."

The thing may have looked like a kangaroo, but it didn't act like one. It was said to have killed and eaten a large dog. There were also reports that the thing had killed and eaten a number of chickens. A search was organized to find this killer kangaroo, but, as usual, the searchers found nothing.

In January, 1949, Louis Staub was driving his bus outside of Grove City, Ohio. He saw something strange in his headlights.

"It's about 5½ feet high, hairy and brownish in color. It had a long pointed head. It leaped a barbed-wire fence and disappeared. It looked like a kangaroo but it appeared to jump on all fours. I'm certain it wasn't a deer."

Phantom kangaroos have been reported in many places in the Midwest.

For many years children in the area of Coon Rapids, Minnesota, reported seeing "a very big bunny." Sometimes the "bunny" was as tall as they were. A woman named Barbara Battmer said that she got a very clear view of two of the creatures hopping through the woods. She said they were not bunnies at all, they were kangaroos.

In most of these reported close encounters with kangaroos, the creature seems pretty harmless. But if you corner it, and try to capture it, then it can turn nasty. At least, that is what a couple of Chicago policemen said in 1974.

Early on the morning of October 18, 1974, a man called the police. He reported that a kangaroo was jumping around on his front porch. The police didn't take the call too seriously. Still, two patrolmen were sent out to investigate.

Not only did the policemen see the kangaroo, they cornered it up a dark alley on Chicago's northwest side. The kangaroo didn't want to be captured and began kicking. The policemen said that they didn't want to shoot the thing, so they just backed off. The kangaroo then hopped over a fence and disappeared down the street.

Over the next few days a lot of people in the area reported a kangaroo. A newsboy selling papers on a corner turned around and saw a

A kangaroo in a zoo is not very frightening. A phantom kangaroo is another matter.

kangaroo standing just a few feet away. "He looked at me, I looked at him, and then away he hopped," the boy said.

The Chicago police got a lot of calls from people who said that the kangaroo was out in their backyards rummaging through their garbage cans. Most of these calls were probably the result of mistaken identity. People heard something—a dog or cat or raccoon rummaging around in the garbage. But with all the kangaroo excitement they assumed it was the kangaroo, and called the police.

The newspapers didn't take the whole thing too seriously. They reported the kangaroo's doings under such headlines as KANGAROO STAYS A JUMP AHEAD OF THE POLICE. But still, people kept right on reporting the thing. Not only that, it began to look as if there was more than one kangaroo around.

While kangaroo sightings continued on Chicago's northwest side, people also began reporting the thing in towns to the west of Chicago.

On the evening of November 2, three young men were driving along Shafer Road in Plano, Illinois. Plano is about fifty miles west of Chicago. They nearly hit the thing.

"We almost ran over it," one of them said. "It jumped onto the road about twenty feet ahead of us . . . It landed on the road near the intersection with the main road and there was no traffic. It sat up on its haunches as kangaroos do, and then jumped over a fence about five feet high and disappeared into the woods."

At almost the same time a couple walking along a Chicago street spotted what they thought was a large dog. Only after it hopped away did they realize it was the kangaroo.

A man in Rensselaer, Indiana, saw the thing on the morning of November 12. It hopped out of a cornfield and up to the drugstore in which he was working. Then it hopped down the street and off into another cornfield. The sighting touched off a search, but no trace of the beast was found.

The man said, "I hope some farmer or somebody else sees it or everybody'll think I'm a nut. But it was a kangaroo . . . I know it was." Within a few days several other people reported seeing the kangaroo in the same area.

By the end of November, the great kangaroo flap had died down. But sightings started up again in Illinois in 1975 and 1976. And in 1976 a Colorado policeman was checking out a kangaroo report, and said that he spotted the creature around some clay pits near Golden, Colorado. As usual, it got away.

Every time there is a rash of kangaroo sightings reporters call the local zoo. Zoo directors get pretty tired of saying that none of their kangaroos have escaped.

There was a 1968 kangaroo flap in Ohio. The director of the Cincinnati Zoo told reporters, "I doubt there's a kangaroo around here on the loose. We had a kangaroo story about two years ago. Never found one. Down the years we've chased after reported black leopards, panthers, and even a polar bear. Anyone seeing the kangaroo, which I doubt exists, should try to keep it in sight and call the zoo."

5

THE HAIRY HANDS

Dartmoor is a rather wild and remote part of England. The people of Dartmoor have many legends about headless ghosts and spectral hounds. Most of these legends are centuries old. But not all of the strange tales go back hundreds of years. Some are fairly recent. One of the most mysterious is the story of the Hairy Hands.

There is a stretch of road between the villages of Postbridge and Two Bridges. It is a rather ordinary piece of road. It runs through slightly rolling moors, and for the most part is fairly straight. Yet during the early years of this century there seem to have been an unusual number of accidents on that road, particularly in the vicinity of the village of Archerton.

At first, the main means of transportation along the road was horsepower. Riders would describe how, suddenly and for an unknown reason, their horses would panic and dash off, often throwing the rider. Pony carts were often used by local farmers. Ponies would veer off without warning, and the farmer would find himself in a ditch with his cart overturned. There were many injuries as the result of such mishaps.

After the bicycle became popular cyclists too seemed to fall victim to unusual accidents on this road. Some said that it felt as if the handlebars were torn out of their control. Bicycles plunged into ditches or crashed into the stone walls which border much of the road.

Cars and buses had more serious accidents. They skidded off the road and into walls. People were sometimes killed in such accidents. A local doctor was riding along the road on a motorcycle. His two children were riding in the sidecar. Then suddenly the motorcycle went

The Hairy Hands, from a woodcut by Theo Brown.

out of control. No one is sure why. There was a terrible crash. The two children were thrown clear, but the doctor was killed.

That piece of road was getting a very bad reputation. Something was wrong with it—but what?

In 1921 a young Army officer was seriously injured when his motorcycle crashed along that same stretch of road. He seemed to have suddenly veered off the road for no reason at all. Later, he recalled what had happened just before the crash. He said that he distinctly saw a pair of large hairy hands clamp down over his own. The hands twisted the motorcycle's handlebars, forcing it off the road.

That story caught the attention of reporters for the London *Daily Mail.* They came down to Dartmoor. The reporters talked to a lot of people who said that they felt the presence of "something" when they went down that stretch of road.

The Hairy Hands became front-page news. Interest was so high that local road authorities felt that they had to do something. They investigated the road. Then they decided that there was indeed something wrong with the road. According to the authorities, there were too many little ups and downs in the road. These could cause vehicles to go out of control. Road repairs were made. But what about the Hairy Hands? The authorities said that was all nonsense.

But the story didn't end with the road repairs. Three years later a woman and her husband parked their trailer near the spot where the

The stretch of road haunted by the Hairy Hands.

Hairy Hands had been reported. That night the woman was awakened by a scratching noise on the window. She said that she saw a large hairy hand clawing at the window. She sensed something evil. The woman slipped out of her bunk and fell to her knees. She made the sign of the cross, and the hand disappeared. But the feeling of evil lingered on. She said that she and her husband never again went to that part of the country.

In the early 1960s rumors about the Hairy Hands were back. Ruth E. St. Leger-Gordon, a collector of Dartmoor folklore, reported she had heard of a strange accident near the fatal spot on the road. A young man was found dead beneath his overturned car. Police could find no reason for the accident to have happened at all.

There were also more rumors about people seeing the Hairy Hands, at a different place on the road.

The Dartmoor folklorist reports that most local people now laugh at tales of the Hairy Hands. But there are still a fair number who insist that there must be "something" to the story. A genuine fear of that section of the road has grown over the years.

6

DEMON DOGS

The most famous of all the Sherlock Holmes stories is the story of "The Hound of the Baskervilles." It is a story about a dog of monstrous size. The dog seems to have supernatural powers. According to legend, it had killed one of the ancestors of the Baskerville family. Many years later it appeared to be on the prowl again, stalking another member of the family.

The great detective Holmes proved that the legendary dog was really a fake. It was large and vicious, but otherwise quite a normal dog. It had been used by the villian to frighten the Baskervilles.

The Hound of the Baskervilles

Sir Arthur Conan Doyle wrote the Sherlock Holmes stories. But the idea of "The Hound of the Baskervilles" is not a completely original one. Legends about such a dog are very common in the British Isles. Many people think that Sir Arthur Conan Doyle got his idea from legends about the Black Dog of Dartmoor. It was supposed to be a huge black creature with blazing eyes. It roamed the lonely roads and moors. If a traveler happened to meet the monster, his only chance was to run for his life. If the demon dog caught him, it would tear him to bits.

Dartmoor isn't the only part of England that was supposed to be visited by demon dogs. There were many legends about the animal seen at a place called Tring in Hartford, England. It was said that the demon dog appeared near a spot where a woman had been hanged for witchcraft. About 150 years ago a man published a report of his meeting with this monster.

The man and his companion were riding home in a cart at night. They were just passing the spot where the hanging had taken place. There was a sudden flash of light.

"What's that?" the man cried out.

"Hush," said his companion. He pulled the horse to a stop.

"I then saw an immense black dog just in front of our horse. It was the strangest-looking creature I ever saw. He was as big as a Newfoundland dog, but very thin and shaggy. He had long ears, a long tail, and eyes like balls of fire. When he opened his mouth we could see long teeth. He seemed to grin at us. In a few minutes the dog disappeared, seeming to

Scene from a movie version of *The Hound of the Baskervilles.*

vanish like a shadow, or to sink into the earth . . ."

Collectors of folklore have heard many similar stories from English country people. There was a Mrs. Jewell who told of her meeting with the Black Dog of Torrington. She said it happened in the 1870s, when she was only about ten years old.

Late at night she was walking down the road with her father. "It was a moonlight night," she said, "and suddenly a sound of something panting came from behind us, and a great black dog, big as a calf, with great shining eyes, came alongside us. I caught at father's hand and cried out. Father said, 'Tis the Black Dog! Hold my hand, don't speak, walk along quietly, and don't cry out.'"

The dog trotted alongside them for about a quarter of a mile. Then father and daughter turned to go into their cottage. The dog did not follow. The girl's father said that he had seen the dog many times before, and it had never harmed anyone.

Mrs. Jewell said that later in life she also saw

the dog several times, but never at close range. She insisted that many other people in the district had seen it, but would not talk about it because they thought that outsiders would not believe them.

The woman who wrote down old Mrs. Jewell's account was Barbara Carbonell. She collected another Black Dog of Torrington story from her own daughter. Her daughter said that in 1932 she and her husband were driving down a road in the Torrington region. Suddenly an enormous black dog appeared in the headlights of their car. The driver slammed on the brakes. But he was quite sure that there was no way to avoid hitting the creature. Somehow there was no crash. When the car stopped and the couple got out to investigate, they could find no trace at all of whatever it was.

On the Isle of Man there is a place called Peel Castle. There is a well-known black dog legend attached to the castle. The creature was called the Moddey Dhoo. Back in the seventeenth century there was a garrison of soldiers stationed at the castle. A huge shaggy black dog used to

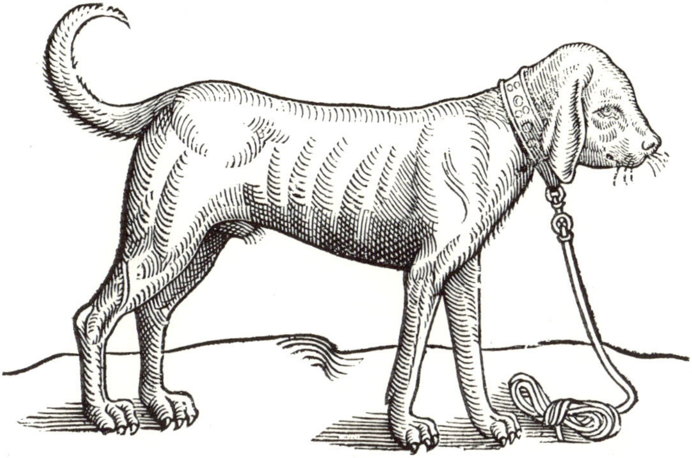

This is an English bloodhound. Could it be mistaken for a demon dog?

come into the guardroom. No one knew who owned the dog, or how it had come into the castle. But the thing was so frightening looking that none of the soldiers had the courage to touch it. So it would just come into the guardroom every once in a while, then disappear.

One day a soldier who had been drinking tried to challenge the beast. He yelled at it, and dared it to follow him up the stairs. Then he ran out of the guardroom and the dog padded out after him. There was a horrible scream. The man staggered back into the room. He was pale and trembling. Worst of all, he seemed to have lost his power of speech. The poor fellow died three days later, but he was never able to reveal what had happened to him. The black dog was never seen again in Peel Castle.

However, in the 1920s and 1930s, several people did report seeing the Moddey Dhoo at other places on the Isle of Man. Seeing the dog was taken to be a sign of bad luck. One man who said he met the dog reported that his father died a short time later.

Throughout the British Isles there is a tradition that graveyards were guarded by a spirit in the form of a black dog. Though the black dog was supposed to protect the souls of those buried in the graveyard from the Devil, it was considered extremely bad luck for any living person to see the dog. In fact, anyone who saw it was supposed to die within a year.

Several old English families are supposed to be cursed with a black dog. Whenever the dog appears, a member of the family dies.

As a rule, one would not care to meet one of these black dogs. But there are a few stories in which mysterious black dogs guarded travelers.

There was a tale told at the beginning of this century about a man named Johnnie Greenwood. One night he had to ride through a wood about a mile long to get to where he was going. At the entrance to the wood a large black dog joined him. It just trotted along by his side. He had no idea where it came from.

Even when it got so dark that he could no longer see the dog, Johnnie knew it was there because he could hear its footsteps. But when he came out of the woods the dog was gone.

That same night Johnnie returned the same way he had come. At the entrance to the wood the dog joined him again. As before, he didn't touch it or speak to it. When he got out of the woods the dog was once again gone.

Years later, two prisoners condemned to be hanged confessed that they had intended to rob and murder Johnnie that night in the wood. But when they saw the dog, they decided that both Johnnie and the dog would be too much to handle, so they left him alone.

As we have seen, phantom dogs can be dangerous, helpful, or just frightening. But no sane person would ever want to meet a whole pack of phantom hounds. For these would most likely be the feared creatures known as the Wish Hounds or the Devil's Dogs.

The Wish Hounds, or the Devil's Dogs, are part of one of the oldest and most persistent of all European legends—the Wild Hunt. The legend runs like this: On certain nights a phantom hunstman, leading a pack of phantom hounds, can be heard, and sometimes seen, racing across the desolate countryside.

In one form or another this legend is told throughout Europe. Often the huntsman is said to be the Devil or some demon. Sometimes he is supposed to be a particularly evil person condemned to ride until Judgment Day without a rest. The dogs are usually described as being black with glowing red eyes. In some versions of the tale, however, the dogs are described as being headless.

According to the legend, anyone unlucky enough to see the Wild Hunt will be torn to pieces by the dogs or otherwise killed. Failing that, the unlucky soul is sure to die within a year.

Belief in the Wish Hounds remained strong until the end of the last century. In England in the 1870s a body was found on the banks of the River Yealm. An inquest was held to find the cause of death. When no obvious cause could be found, the jury wanted to say that the man was "struck down by the phantom hunt" or met "death by supernatural agency." With some difficulty the jury was persuaded to return a more ordinary verdict of "accidental death."

In recent years, belief in the Wild Hunt appears to have weakened. But up until the 1950s, at least, there were still people who said they could hear the barking and yelping of the phantom hounds on dark and stormy nights.

People didn't want to go out and see if the huntsman and his pack were really out there. They knew too many stories about what was supposed to have happened to those who did see the Wild Hunt.

But from time to time there was a story about someone who escaped the demon hunter and his phantom hounds.

About a century ago a tale of a poor but very lucky herdsman was told in the west of England.

The herdsman was riding home one night. In the distance he heard the baying of the Devil's Dogs. He knew he had several miles to go before he reached the safety of his home. He rode as fast as he could, but the phantom pack was gaining on him. When he turned around he could see them coming up behind him. The hunter had horns and a tail, just as the Devil is usually pictured. The dogs were black and snorted fire. The noise they made was horrible.

There was no shelter, no place where the herdsman could hide. Then suddenly he had a thought. He stopped his horse, jumped off and fell to his knees in prayer. The dogs that were just about to pounce on him held back, howling more loudly than ever. The demon hunter looked at him and said, "The boy prays." At that, they all turned off in pursuit of some other soul.

7

BIG-BIG BIRD

The American Indians have a legend about a creature called the Thunderbird. The Thunderbird is supposed to be gigantic. According to some legends, it could darken the entire sky as it flew by.

Most people think that the Thunderbird is completely a legend. It has been suggested that the idea of the Thunderbird was based on the condor. The condor is a very large vulture-like bird. It has a wingspan of from six to eight feet. The condor was once found throughout the American West. Today it is very rare. It lives only in the mountains of California. It is so rare that many scientists fear that it will soon become extinct. A somewhat larger condor lives in South America. But neither bird is anywhere near the size of the Thunderbird of Indian legend.

There are a few people who claim that the Thunderbird is more than a legend. They say that the stories are based on a gigantic, but unknown, bird. This bird may have existed until just a short time ago. And some think it may still exist today.

Unfortunately, the best piece of evidence for the existence of the Thunderbird has been lost. Perhaps it never even existed.

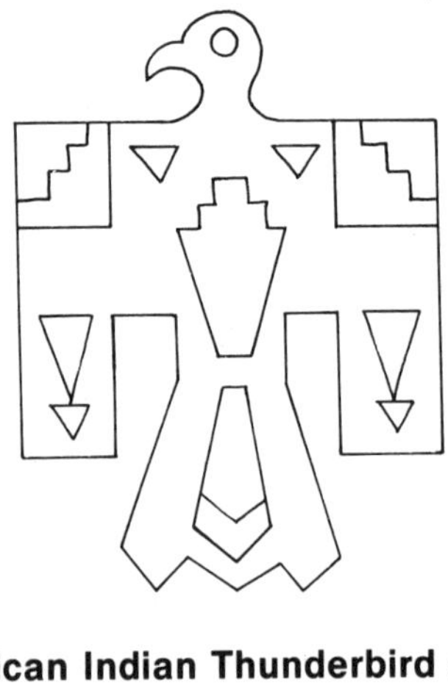

American Indian Thunderbird design

The condor

Here is the story. In 1886, a group of ranchers from Tombstone, Arizona, shot and killed a monster bird. They nailed it up, wings outstretched, on a barn. Then six men stood in front of the bird with their arms out, fingertips touching. This was to give some idea of the bird's size. Six average-sized men with outstretched arms would cover a distance of between thirty and thirty-six feet.

Now this astonishing scene is supposed to

have been photographed. And the photograph was supposed to have been printed in the Tombstone newspaper. The paper had a very appropriate name, the Tombstone *Epitaph.* A lot of people say that they have seen the picture. The problem is that no one seems to be able to *find* it. A check of the files of the Tombstone *Epitaph,* which go back to about that time, reveal no trace of such a photograph.

One well-known monster hunter said that he had a copy of the original picture in his files. But he loaned it out, and it was never returned. To whom did he loan it? He couldn't remember.

There is another Big-Big Bird story from Tombstone that was supposed to have taken place at about the same time. It may be just another version of the original story. This time, however, the monster is winged, but has no feathers. It is supposed to have been smooth and hairless, its enormous jaws lined with razor-sharp teeth. The wings, which measured up to 160 feet, were thin membranes of skin. This creature was supposed to have been shot, or at least seen, in the Tombstone area around 1890.

The whole idea could be dismissed as just a wilder version of an already wild legend—except for one thing. This creature sounds more like one of the ancient flying reptiles called pterodactyls than it does like a bird. Pterodactyl-type creatures had the largest wingspread of any flying creature ever known. Actually, the pterodactyls probably didn't really fly. They would just glide along on air currents. They were very light, but their huge wings—30 or 40 feet from tip to tip—would keep them up in the air.

The trouble is that pterodactyls died out at

Some think the Thunderbird was some kind of giant flying reptile.

about the same time the dinosaurs did—60 million years ago.

Giant bird stories come mainly from the American West. But there are a few interesting accounts from the East as well. In May, 1961, there was a report by the pilot of a private plane who was flying in New York State's Hudson Valley. He spotted what appeared to be another and slightly larger plane nearby. Suddenly this "plane" turned and tried to chase him. The pilot was surprised and frightened, but he circled back to try and get a closer look at the hostile plane. Then he noticed that the other "plane" was flapping its wings. It wasn't a plane at all; it was a gigantic bird. The pilot had seen enough. He flew off in a hurry.

There are frequent tales of planes crashing because of encounters with giant birds. There is no real evidence to support any of these rumors, but the stories continue to exist.

Probably the most celebrated case took place in November, 1962. A United Airlines jet crashed in a wooded area of Maryland near Washington,

D.C. There were no survivors in the crash. However, there were traces of blood and feathers found in the wreckage. Investigators decided that the plane must have run into a flock of birds shortly before it crashed. Perhaps the birds were even in some way responsible for the crash. Collisions with birds have been blamed for other plane crashes.

But some monster hunters noticed that scratches and gouges had been found on the tail assembly of the plane. They suggested that the plane had run into a Thunderbird. That angered the monster bird, which then turned and attacked the plane, sending it to its doom.

Why had the pilot not radioed information about his collision with a giant bird before the crash? Why had a bird of that size not been tracked on radar? Where is the monster bird hiding now? Questions like that have no answers.

8

THE DOVER DEMON

Some monsters are reported frequently. They become legends. Other are seen only a few times. Then they seem to disappear. The Dover Demon was that sort of creature. But it certainly created enough excitement when it was reported.

The time was April 21 and 22, 1977. The place was the pretty town of Dover, Massachusetts, about fifteen miles southwest of Boston.

At about 10:30 in the evening of April 21, three seventeen-year-olds were out for a ride. Bill Bartlett was driving. Bill saw something creeping along a low wall at the side of the road. At first, he thought it was a cat. Then the headlights hit it and he got a good look.

The thing had a huge head with shining orange eyes. The rest of the body was small and skinny in comparison. It had long fingers and toes. The creature appeared to be hairless with a rough, peach-colored skin. He estimated that it would stand about four feet tall.

Bartlett only saw it for an instant, as the car lights flashed on it.

"Did you see that?" he yelled to the two passengers. The other two boys had been talking, and not looking out the window, so they didn't see a thing. But they wanted to. Bill was frightened, but the others persuaded him to drive back to the place where he had seen the thing. If it had ever been there, it was gone by the time they got back.

A little less then two hours later a fifteen-year-old named John Baxter was walking home. He saw a small figure coming down the street. He thought it was a friend of his who was quite short. He called out to the figure, but got no answer.

When he tried to get close to it, the figure

took off and ran into a wooded area. John tried to follow it. It stopped about thirty feet away from him. In the darkness he could only make out a shadowy form.

He said the figure had a body like a monkey, but a big "figure eight"-shaped head. He could see its eyes, but no other features. It was staring at him. This made John feel very uneasy. He backed away carefully and then he ran.

Both Bill Bartlett and John Baxter made drawings of what they saw—or what they said they saw. The drawings looked like they were of the same creature. Both boys also said that they had not heard the other's story before they made the drawings.

The next evening two other teenagers, Will Taintor and Abby Brabham, said they got a glimpse of the creature. They were driving along and picked up something in the headlights on the side of the road. The thing was crouched on all fours. Abby described it as having a very large head and a thin, monkey-like body. She could not see any mouth or nose, but its large eyes seemed to glow with a green-

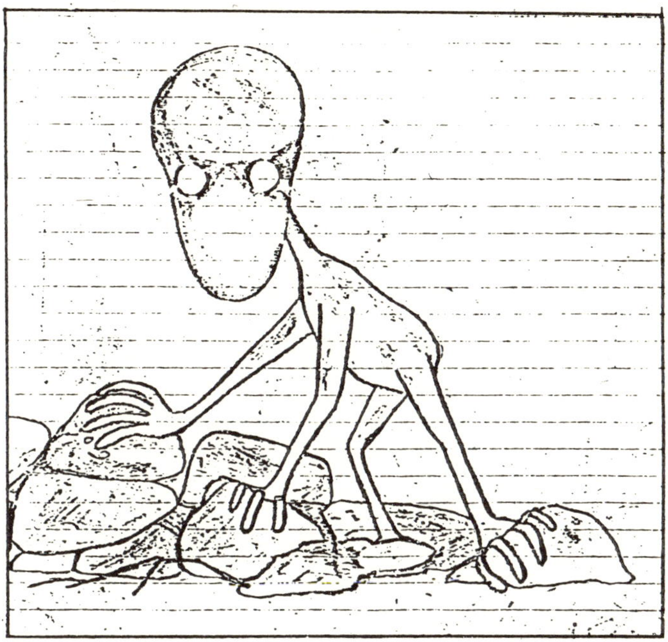

Bill Bartlett drew this picture of the Dover Demon.

ish light. Will only got a fleeting glimpse of the figure. He had the impression of something with a large head, and tan body.

The story got into the newspapers, and the thing was dubbed the Dover Demon.

No one else ever reported seeing the Dover Demon. No physical evidence of its existence was ever produced. A lot of people talked to the

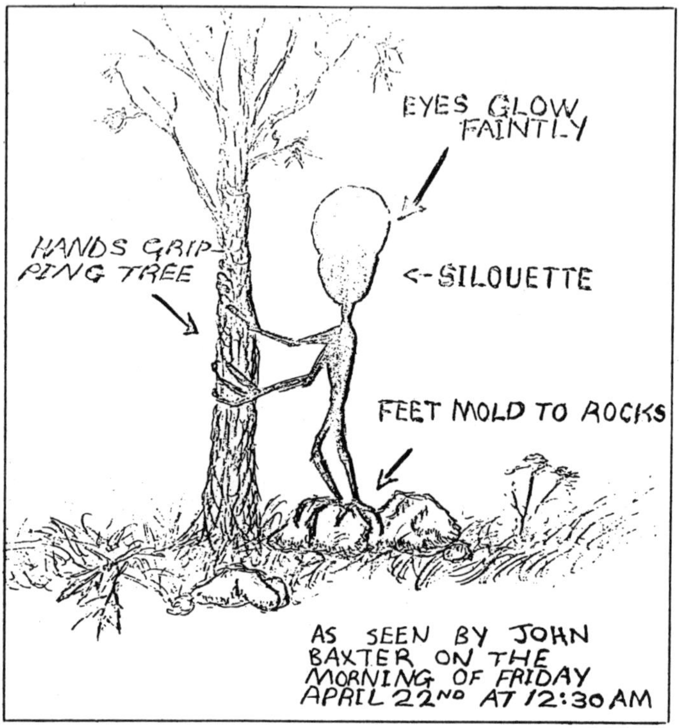

This is John Baxter's drawing of the figure he said he saw.

four young witnesses about their strange encounters. A few thought it was all a hoax. Most people got the feeling that the witnesses were telling the truth. But even if they were telling the truth, as far as they knew it, that does not mean that they actually saw a strange little creature with a large head and skinny body. They may have seen something quite ordinary—a cat or dog perhaps. It was night. No one really got a good close-up look at the creature. They may have just gotten excited and made a mistake about what they saw. At least one of the witnesses knew about the other sightings before he made his report. People often see strange things—or think that they do—especially at night.

But what if it wasn't a hoax or a mistake? What could the Dover Demon be?

A lot of people who are interested in the subject are also interested in UFOs. They think that the Dover Demon might be something that came out of a UFO, though there had been no important UFO sightings around Dover at that time.

Then someone suggested that the Dover Demon might be a Mannegishi. The Mannegishi are creatures of the mythology of the Cree Indians of Canada. They are supposed to be little people with round heads and no noses. They have long thin arms and legs. Their main purpose in life, according to Cree legends, is to play jokes on the big people.

9
THE BIGGEST SNAKE

How long can a snake grow? According to the *Guinness Book of World Records,* the longest and heaviest of all snakes is the anaconda of South America. The book says that a 37½-foot anaconda was "reliably reported" to have been killed on the upper Orinoco River in eastern Columbia. That snake should have weighed about 1,000 pounds.

A 33½-foot anaconda was killed in southeastern Columbia in November, 1956.

A 1,000-pound, 37½-foot snake is *enormous.* Even a 20-foot snake is a giant, and among anacondas the 20-foot length is fairly common. But there are rumors of anacondas and other

Major Percy Fawcett's meeting with a 62-foot anaconda, from a drawing by his son.

snakes which are far, far larger.

Take the story of Major Percy Fawcett, a British Army officer and frequent traveler in the Amazon jungles of South America. He had heard stories of 50- and 60-foot anacondas. But he didn't believe them. Then one day early in 1907, Major Fawcett and several local Indians were in a canoe drifting along the Rio Abuna river. Suddenly, a giant triangular head appeared practically underneath the boat. It was a monstrous anaconda. The creature slithered out of the water and onto the bank. Fawcett didn't stand around watching it. He grabbed his rifle and shot it. He made a rough measurement of the creature. It turned out to be 62 feet long. It also had a terrible odor. "Everything about this snake was repulsive," Fawcett commented.

Fawcett said that later he heard of even larger anacondas.

When Fawcett got back to London a lot of people called him a liar because of his 62-foot snake story. But if he was a liar, he wasn't the only one.

The Belgian naturalist, Bernard Heuvelmans, has a long-time interest in strange, unusual, and unknown animals. He met a Frenchman named Serge Bonacase, who had been in Brazil in 1947. Bonacase told the naturalist an astonishing story.

He said he was with a group of Frenchmen and Brazilians that spotted an anaconda asleep in the grass. They got about twenty yards away from it and fired their rifles at it several times. Only after they killed it did they realize how enormous it was. "When we walked along the whole length of its body it seemed as if it would never end."

What Bonacase found most impressive was the thing's head. To demonstrate the size of the head, Bonacase stretched out his arms in front of himself, with his hands together. This formed a triangle with two-foot sides and an 18-inch base.

Bonacase's group didn't have anything to measure the snake with except a piece of string about three feet long. Using it, they estimated that the creature was between 72 and 75 feet in length.

None of the group had a camera. There was no possibility of carrying back a snake of that size and weight. But why didn't they bring back its skin, or head? Bonacase said no one thought it would be worth the trouble. They didn't think there was anything that unusual about the creature.

"The Brazilian officials who had spent much of their lives in this country did not seem to be particularly surprised. As for me, I had heard so many tales of giant snakes that I supposed the whole of the Amazon was crawling with monsters of this size."

Try to imagine a snake 75 or 80 feet long.

That is almost four times as long as the longest snake you have ever seen, or have ever seen a picture of. The longest snake kept in a zoo was a mere 22 feet. A 75- or 80-foot anaconda is a real monster.

And there is more. There are rumors of another, even larger snake in South America. It is supposed to be some sort of water snake that lives in the Amazon River and its tributaries. Stories make the thing sound so big that it has been called an inland sea serpent.

A priest, Father Victor Heinz, reported seeing this monster twice. The first time was on May 22, 1922. He was riding in a canoe down the Amazon when he saw a giant water snake drifting quietly and gently downstream. "I reckoned that its body was as thick as an oil-drum and its visible length was some 80 feet."

Father Heinz' next meeting with the monster came in 1929. He was on the river at night. Suddenly, his crew became very frightened. They began to row madly toward shore.

"What is it?" Father Heinz cried.

"There is a big animal," they muttered, very excited.

The giant anaconda of South America

At the same moment he heard the water move. It sounded as if a steamboat was passing. Then he saw two bluish-green lights several feet above the water. He thought they were lights on a riverboat. The two lights, however, came from the monster's eyes which glowed in the dark. The monster simply avoided Father Heinz' canoe and swam over to the other side of the river.

Glowing eyes figure in many accounts of this giant water snake. On July 6, 1930, a Portuguese merchant named Reymondo Zima was going down the river at night in his motorboat. He was looking for a house on the right bank. He saw a light near the shore. Thinking it was the house, he steered toward it. Then he switched on his own searchlight. Suddenly, the light began charging his boat at a high speed. It turned out to be a giant water snake, which had only one glowing eye. Zima assumed that the animal had somehow lost the other eye. He thought the creature had mistaken his searchlight for the eye of a fellow snake. The creature nearly overturned Zima's little boat, but he managed to make it safely to shore.

There have been many stories about giant snakes attacking people and other animals.

If the man in this drawing is six feet tall, imagine the length of the giant snake.

Another priest, Father Protesius Frickel, said he saw one of the monsters lying in the water near the bank. He got within about a dozen steps of the beast, but it did not move. "It's eyes," he wrote, "were as large as plates."

In addition to the many reports of giant water snake sightings, there are also supposed to have been two photographs. The first was taken in 1933. The group that took the photo said that they had killed the monster with a machine gun. Before it died, however, it lifted its head 30 feet in the air. When it fell it crushed bushes and trees. Four men were unable to lift the dead creature's head.

The second photograph was taken in 1948. This monster was said to have crawled ashore and tried to hide in an old fort. But it was killed, though it took 500 machine gun bullets to do the job. The dead snake was measured at 115 feet.

Where are these astonishing photographs? They were supposed to have been published in a newspaper in Rio de Janeiro. But no one seems to know which paper or where the original photos are.

Unless these photographs are found, or a skull, a skin, or a whole snake turns up, the giant water snake of the Amazon will just have to remain another of the world's elusive monsters.

10
THE TAZELWORM

As far as monsters go, the tazelworm really isn't too much. It is only supposed to be about two or three feet long. There are stories that the bite of the tazelworm is highly poisonous. It has been said that the creature is so poisonous that even its breath can kill you. According to legend, the tazelworm is very mean, and will attack anything that moves.

But even people who believe in the tazelworm do not believe all of these stories.

The most responsible beliefs about the tazelworm are this: It is a largish lizard, with two or four short legs. It may have a poisonous bite, but this is not absolutely certain. Far from being aggressive, the beast is very shy, though, like other animals, it will attack if cornered.

In fact, it is its very shyness that makes the tazelworm so interesting and, in a way, makes it a monster. For the tazelworm, if it exists at all, is a farily large creature that has remained undetected by scientists, right in the middle of Europe. It would be the largest lizard in Europe, and one of the largest in the whole world.

If the tazelworm exists, it would be proof that large and unusual-looking animals can remain undetected in the modern world. If the tazelworm exists, it would strengthen the case for the existence of other monsters. After all, if the tazelworm could escape detection, so could other animals.

But does the tazelworm exist? That is the problem. As far as monsters go, the evidence for the tazelworm is very good.

The creature is supposed to live in the valleys of the Swiss, Bavarian, and Austrian alps. It is known by many different names. "Tazelworm" is the most common. The name means "worm with feet." It has also been called a tunnel

Drawing of the tazelworm, from a Bavarian hunting manual of 1836.

worm, a jumping worm, or a mountain stump. Of course, it is not a worm at all, but some sort of lizard.

Stories about the tazelworm are so common that it was included in an 1861 book on the animals of the Alps. The author said the creature was thick, from three to six feet long, had two short legs, and generally appeared before storms after a long dry spell.

The author added, "Many honest and respectable people swear that they have seen it with their own eyes." The author also said that in 1828 a Swiss peasant found a dead tazelworm. The creature's skeleton was sent to the University at Heidelberg, in Germany. But whether it arrived or not, no one seems to know, for all trace of the skeleton was lost.

In the 1930s a scientific society and some

local newspapers put out a call for people who had seen the beast. More than sixty witnesses stepped forward. In general, the witnesses agreed as to the size and shape of what they had seen. Some said the thing had four very tiny legs, while others said it had no back legs at all. (Two-legged lizards are not unknown.) Most of the witnesses said it had scales, and hissed like a snake. A few said that it was able to jump two or three yards. How it was able to accomplish this with tiny legs, or no back legs at all, was not explained.

One hunter said he saw the thing in 1909. Knowing that it was supposed to be poisonous, he approached with great caution. Suddenly, the beast jumped at him. He drew his hunting knife and tried to stab it, but the creature's scales were so thick that the blade would barely penetrate. After a couple of attacks the tazel-worm retreated into a hole in the ground. The stunned hunter was not able to find it again.

An Austrian schoolteacher was doing a little mountain climbing in April, 1929. He stopped for a moment to rest and saw what he called

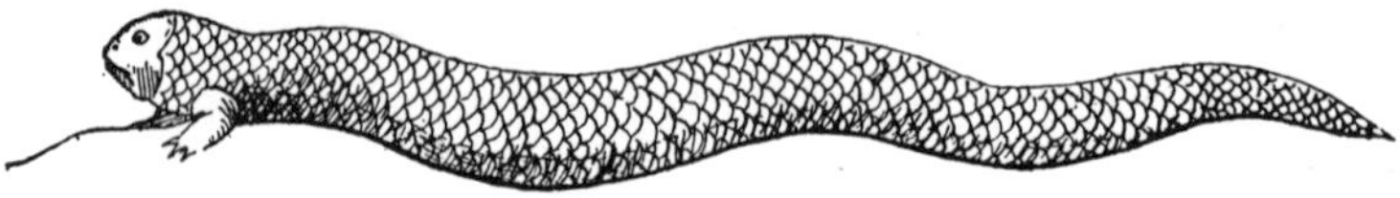

The tazelworm, as shown in an 1841 Swiss almanac.

a "snake-like animal" sprawled out on the ground.

"It did not move," he said, "but kept staring at me with its remarkably large eyes. I know every one of our animals at first glance and knew that I faced one that is unknown to science, the tazelworm. Excited, joyful, but at the same time somewhat fearful, I tried to grab the animal but I was too late."

For a rather stumpy looking animal, the tazelworm moved with remarkable speed. It disappeared down a hole in the ground. The disappointed schoolteacher remarked, "I am certain that it was not my imagination that let me see the animal, but that I observed with a clear head."

So another chance to prove the existence of the tazelworm skipped or slithered away. In 1934, a Swiss photographer said he snapped a picture of the beast. The picture was published in the newspapers, but frankly it looks phony.

The animal has been so hard to catch that there are many skeptics who say that it does not exist at all. They say that perhaps the people are seeing something else. One suggestion was that people might be seeing a badger that had some kind of skin condition that made it hairless and scaly looking. Badgers live in holes in the ground. They have very short legs, and can make hissing sounds. Usually badgers hide, but they can become very aggressive when they think they are being threatened.

Nonsense, say the witnesses. They know the difference between a strange-looking lizard and a bald badger.

So the argument goes on. It will go on until someone actually catches a tazelworm, or until no one reports seeing a tazelworm for so many years that people forget about it.

The same kind of argument goes on about other monsters as well.

11

THE INVISIBLE KILLERS

Is someone or something going around the country killing cows and sheep, and then cutting them up?

There are a lot of people who think so.

The so-called cattle mutilation mystery is one of the goriest, and most discussed, mysteries in America today. There have been several conferences on the subject. There is an organization devoted to solving it. There is even a magazine about the cattle mutilation mystery.

Current interest in the subject began in 1974 in Nebraska and South Dakota. Ranchers would find some of their cattle dead on the range.

There was no obvious cause of death. Worse yet, parts of the animal might be missing. There were no footprints or other evidence to hint at what had happened or why.

There was a real panic on the ranches. Ranchers began patrolling their ranges at night with guns. They wanted to catch whoever or whatever was responsible. They never caught anything; they never even saw anything.

The police were called in. So were veterinarians. Some veterinarians said that there was really no mystery at all. The cattle, they said, had died natural deaths. Cattle, like other living things, die for a variety of reasons. There was no evidence they had been specially killed. What about the mutilations? The veterinarians said that small predatory animals like weasels might have gotten to the dead animals. These animals were so small and light that they would leave no footprints.

Cattle rustlers might also account for some of the deaths. Most people think that cattle rustling is only a part of the Old West. This isn't true. With the price of beef as high as it is, stealing cattle has become a very profitable business.

Still another possibility is that some of the ranchers might be killing or mutilating their own cattle. They might do this for the insurance money. Insurance companies will pay for cattle that die accidental deaths, but not for cattle that die natural deaths.

These possible explanations calmed the fears of the Nebraska and South Dakota ranchers. The scare died away after a few months. But since then cattle mutilation scares have cropped up in Texas, Arizona, and elsewhere.

The story is not a new one. People have been collecting accounts of mysterious cattle deaths for many years. Reports of similar incidents have come from many other countries, particularly Great Britain.

In addition to the ordinary explanations, other far stranger explanations have been offered for the mysterious deaths. One is that the animals have been killed by some kind of Devil's cult. It has been suggested that killing cattle is part of the ritual.

UFOs have often been blamed as the source of the phantom cattle killers. Why would creatures from other planets want to go around killing earthly cattle? No one has any reasonable suggestions. But people like to lump mysteries together, even if they have nothing to do with one another.

And then there is the monster explanation. There have been some vague reports that a monster has been seen in areas where the killings have taken place. In Nebraska and South Dakota it was called "the Thing." It was supposed to be a two-legged Bigfoot-like creature.

Now we must admit that most monster reports are hard to pin down. But these reports were even more difficult to check than most. No one seemed to know exactly who had seen "the Thing," or when or exactly where. There just seemed to be sort of a general feeling that a monster of some kind must be responsible, and no one really saw anything.

But what if the mysterious cattle killing monster was invisible? This explanation has been seriously suggested several times. And some people even say that there is evidence of the existence of an invisible monster.

One of the strangest, and spookiest, invisible monster stories appeared in the December, 1977, issue of *Fate* magazine. It is about what is supposed to have happened on two small farms located in a northern Michigan game preserve. The account was written by Bradley Earl Ayers, who had visited the farms and talked to the witnesses.

The farmers were given the names Art Dahl and Henry Dubois, though these were not their real names.

The trouble seemed to begin on the Dubois farm in 1971. A calf was mysteriously killed. No one thought too much of it. There are bears, and other large animals, in the area. They might have been responsible. Still, no one found any tracks.

Over the next few years there were a few more odd incidents. At first, no one connected them. Then in 1976 several of Dubois' pigs were killed. Whatever had killed them seemed to be enormously strong.

The local game warden was called in. There was nothing he could do because he couldn't find any evidence that any of the animals he knew of killed the pigs. As usual, there were no footprints.

Dubois then asked for help from his neighbor, Art Dahl. The two men, aided by their wives and families, began patrolling the farm at night. They didn't see or hear anything unusual until early in the morning of August 19.

Dubois and Dahl had been sitting up all night waiting for something to happen. They were both armed. First, they saw some strange lights in the sky. A couple of hours passed. Then they heard something coming through the marsh. It was coming right for the camper in which the men were sitting. A large dog the men had brought with them cowered under the camper. They heard a sound which they described as a "screech-growl." Dahl said it was "half-human and half-animal." It was the strangest thing he had ever heard. They saw a shadowy mass coming out of the marsh. But they never did get a good look at it, for whatever it was quickly backed off and disappeared.

The men were scared, but they investigated anyway. They found no footprints, no broken branches—nothing.

Things on the Dubois and Dahl farms were normal for the rest of the year. But the following year, whatever it was seemed to be back again.

Dubois' brother Frank was out hunting. In the middle of the marsh he heard something following him. He couldn't see anything, but he could hear something moving through the trees. He also just had a feeling that something large was out there. It was a feeling that something was hunting him! He fired his gun several times. But the thing wouldn't go away. He was scared half to death. Finally, he got out of the marsh and ran to his brother's house. He swore he would never go into the marsh again, for anything.

A few days after his brother's fright, Dubois himself decided to explore the marsh once again. He had the same sort of experience. He heard and felt something following him. He even heard the terrifying "screech-growl" again.

But he saw nothing. Since it was beginning to get dark he decided to get out of the marsh. He didn't want to be alone and meet whatever it was in the dark.

Strange deaths and mutilations of animals continued at the Michigan farms and are still reported from other parts of the country.

So there you have a thoroughly modern monster tale. What really happened? Well, the whole thing could be made up. Without names and addresses, there is no way of checking. Perhaps nothing out of the ordinary took place. Dubois and Dahl may just have become over-excited. They may have exaggerated a bit. Even people who are trying to be completely honest exaggerate, particularly if they have been frightened.

Whatever it was, or wasn't, it does show that an awful lot of people today still believe in monsters. We really do fear that there might be something terrifying and unknown prowling around out there, just beyond the light of our campfire.

12

GOATMAN AND THE GRUNCHES

Imagine this—a young couple drives out to some deserted road. It is a spot that people call "lovers' lane." They park the car and turn out the lights. Then suddenly, without any warning, a great hairy thing rushes out of the woods and begins beating on the windows and doors of the car. For a moment the couple are too surprised and terrified to do anything. Then the driver starts the car, and drives away as fast as he can. Over the roar of the motor the couple can hear the monster screaming in rage.

Perhaps you think that's funny. A lot of people think the story is funny when they first hear it. But you wouldn't think it was funny if it happened to you. The fact is that many, many people have reported having that sort of an experience over the past few years.

While the basic story remains the same, the tale of the monster of lovers' lane has been told with many different variations. And there are different local names for the monster in different parts of the country.

In northern Prince Georges County, Maryland, the thing is called Goatman. It is described as looking like a creature that is half-man and half-goat—the legs and feet of a goat, the upper body of a human being, and the horns of a goat. Anyone familiar with the beliefs of the ancient Greeks and Romans will recognize that figure. It sounds like a description of the nature god Pan, or of those wild nature spirits called *satyrs.* It also sounds very much like one of the more common descriptions of the Devil.

There are different opinions about what Goatman is. Some say that he is a supernatural spirit like the *satyrs* or the Devil. There are others who believe that he is real. They even say

Goatman is described as being half-man, half-goat—like the nature god called Pan.

they know where the Goatman came from.

Goatman, according to this version of the story, was a scientist who worked at the National Agricultural Research Center, which is located in Prince Georges County. The scientist was supposed to have been doing some kind of research with goats. Then something went wrong with the experiments, and the scientist slowly turned into the half-goat, half-human monster called Goatman. Goatman retreated into the woods where he hides most of the time.

Goatman has developed a hatred for all other creatures. He is reported to have attacked parked cars with an axe. Though there is no report that Goatman has ever killed a human being, there are reports that he has killed a number of dogs. In fact, every time a dog is found dead under mysterious circumstances, someone will say "Goatman did it."

A reporter who went to investigate the Goatman story found that local high school students would sometimes spray-paint walls or trees with these words: "Goatman was here."

Down in New Orleans there are many tales

Pan, as shown in an old German drawing. Is Goatman a kind of spirit like Pan?

about a similar creature or creatures. But here they are called the Grunches. No one is really sure what the Grunches are. But most local teenagers will insist that they are "real" creatures, not spirits, spooks, or otherwise supernatural beings.

They live on a deserted stretch of road known as Grunch Road. This road is also a popular lovers' lane. When the Grunches spy a parked car, they try to frighten it away by throwing rocks. If that doesn't work, they come screaming out of the woods and begin beating on the car with their fists. That is sure to send people off in a terrible fright.

Grunches are impossible to locate in the daylight. In fact, no one seems exactly sure where they live. When an investigator from the University of New Orleans went out in search of the Grunches, she was given at least eight different locations for "Grunch Road." Needless to say, she never found a Grunch.

But the goatlike monster isn't the only terror of lovers' lane. Consider this report that comes from the town of Elfers, Florida. Four teenagers left a dance. They drove their car down to a dark deserted road and parked. Then they noticed an awful smell. They looked around to see where the smell was coming from. What they saw nearly frightened them to death. It was an animal about the size of a large chimpanzee.

But the creature was green, and it had glowing green eyes. The thing ran out of the woods and jumped on the hood of the car.

"Then we panicked!" said the driver. "I started the motor and the thing jumped off and ran back into the woods. We tore like blazes back to the dance we were supposed to be attending."

There is the report by two young couples who said that they were sitting in a parked car near Decatur, Illinois, on September 22, 1965. They saw a hairy monster about the size of a large man come out of the darkness and toward the car. The creature didn't do anything; it didn't have to. The young people were so badly frightened by the sight of it that they drove off at once.

Later, the two boys said they returned to the spot, but found nothing. The police were called in. They didn't find anything either. The police didn't necessarily believe the monster story, but they didn't necessarily disbelieve it either. "We don't know what they saw," said one policeman. "But they appear to have been well-frightened."

A young couple from Chittyville, Illinois, was also well-frightened on the evening of August 11, 1967. They were sitting in their car when something really huge came out of the woods. They described the thing as being about ten feet tall, "with a head as large as a steering wheel and a dark hairy face." This gigantic creature did nothing more than throw some dirt through an open window of the car. The couple didn't hang around to find out what else it might do.

This is just a sampling, and a small one, of the types of monsters that are supposed to haunt dark and lonely roads. If the accounts are to be believed, then many young people who have gone out for a little privacy got some very strange company instead.

INDEX